Champaign County Historical Archives
Historical Publications Series
Number Five

IVESDALE

A photographic essay by Raymond Bial

Champaign County Historical Archives / The Urbana Free Library

Urbana, Illinois

Library of Congress Catalog Card Number: 82-73325

ISBN: 0-9609646-0-6

Champaign County Historical Archives
The Urbana Free Library
201 South Race Street
Urbana, Illinois 61801

Manufactured in the United States of America

IVESDALE

PREFACE

Ivesdale: A Photographic Essay is the result of a great deal of cooperative effort. Among the organizations involved at one stage or another are the Illinois Humanities Council, the Illinois Arts Council, the Illinois Historical Survey of the University of Illinois, the Champaign County Historical Museum, and the Champaign Public Library, as well as the Champaign County Historical Archives of The Urbana Free Library.

The "Ivesdale Photographic Project," upon which this book is based, was funded in part by the Illinois Humanities Council and the National Endowment for the Humanities. It was designed to picture the people of a small Illinois community at a single moment in time. Ivesdale was selected largely because it represents a thriving farm village in Champaign County – a functioning individual community largely independent of nearby cities.

Publication of the book has been made possible in part by a grant from the Illinois Arts Council and the National Endowment for the Arts. Additional support came from the Lily Gara fund at The Urbana Free Library. In preparing the book, the Archives' intent has been to make every necessary effort to provide high quality reproductions of an unusually fine group of photographs.

Prior publications of The Champaign County Historical Archives include four reproductions of scarce or unique early books and maps, including the *Combined 1893, 1913 and 1929 Atlases of Champaign County*, the Alexander Bowman 1858 map of Champaign County, the *Early History and Pioneers of Champaign County* (1891 edition), and the Alexander Bowman 1863 map of Champaign County. With the publication of *Ivesdale: A Photographic Essay* the Archives expands its publications series by adding what it hopes will be only the first of a number of original works on the history and people of Champaign County, Illinois.

Frederick A. Schlipf
Executive Director
The Urbana Free Library

INTRODUCTION

SITUATED in the southwest corner of Champaign County, the town of Ivesdale consists of a Co-op grain elevator, a cafe that opened during World War II, a hardware store owned and operated by the mayor, St. Joseph Catholic Church, a bank, a Standard gas station, two taverns, and the Knights of Columbus hall. The entire business district fits comfortably into one abbreviated block just south of the elevator and the Wabash railroad tracks.

Quietly clustered around this single main street, beneath a canopy of shade trees, are seventy or so houses. During October, when these photographs were made, virtually all of the homes are decorated for Halloween with paper skeletons or flying witches. Jack-o-lanterns grin from every porch.

However, the island of trees that encompasses the town spreads for no more than four blocks in any direction before it abruptly gives way to farmland – the ocean of corn and soybeans that stretches from Ohio through Iowa.

Settled in 1864 by W. H. Johnson and his family, the town was originally called "Norey" in honor of the Johnsons' daughter, Nora. Later the name was changed to "Ivesdale" after a Mr. Ives, a local landowner. It has also been referred to as "Little Ireland." Many of the first residents were Irish immigrants who came to the area around LaSalle and Peru, Illinois, to dig a canal and ended up settling in Champaign County.

Surrounded by rich black soil, the town has traditionally catered to farming. Although a few residents commute to Champaign, Urbana, or Decatur, the Co-op continues to be the most important enterprise in the community.

In the autumn, area farmers haul their corn and soybeans to the Co-op office where the crops are weighed and moisture samples taken. Then the loads are dumped at the elevator down the road.

Farmers also buy fertilizer and other supplies through the Co-op. They purchase tools from the hardware store, have equipment repaired at the blacksmith shop, or make deposits at the bank. Around lunchtime they drift into the Kirwan Cafe and during slack hours frequently socialize in one of the taverns (with TV blaring a soap opera overhead). The local bars are an important aspect of Ivesdale life. During the years when taverns in other towns were closed on Sundays, Ivesdale achieved a certain notoriety as the only "wet town" in the county.

Within the town itself, the church has always been the primary social organization. Unlike other farm towns in the Corn Belt which are largely Protestant, Ivesdale is predominantly Irish Catholic. The parish managed to support a parochial school until 1958, and church events still involve the whole town as a matter of course. The Annual Costume Contest and Wiener Roast, for example, not only draws most townspeople, but 91 children competed in homemade costumes in the 1979 contest. The church also sponsors other social events such as Chili Suppers and has a very active chapter of the Knights of Columbus.

Unlike many farm towns in the Midwest that have seen their youth drawn off to nearby cities, Ivesdale is still home to a number of families. During the day the children are off to the elementary or high school in Bement, but mid-afternoon the yellow bus lumbers back to deposit small groups at several strategic corners. From there the children hustle home only to return minutes later on bicycles or on foot to buy Baby Ruth candy bars at the cafe or play touch football.

Ivesdale also has many older residents – several in their eighties – who have spent all or the majority of their lives in the town and who can relate a running, eyewitness account of everything that has happened in Ivesdale since Teddy Roosevelt became president and the first automobile sputtered into town. This would, of course, be impossible in larger cities, but in Ivesdale the life of a single individual can easily encompass every significant event.

Spending much of their time within their homes, the older folks can occasionally be seen going to fetch the mail or puttering in their gardens. They do not completely define Ivesdale, but beneath the surface, from what they hold in memory, they most embody the history and character of the town.

In undertaking this study, rather than simply "covering" the town, I tried to do portraits that would individually stand as character studies and that would collectively form an essay on Ivesdale.

Other photographers might have tried to convey the "story" of this small, low-key town. However, in seeking the essence of the town, I avoided a photojournalistic approach. I felt that candid photographs, because of their dramatic nature, would be inappropriate to Ivesdale, and that extensive narration should be unnecessary.

In most cases, I allowed people to present themselves squarely to the camera. I felt that forthright images, with more or less indirect subtleties, would be most suggestive of the actual temperament of this small town on the Illinois plains.

Raymond Bial

Plate 1

Paul Giblin, Postmaster

Plate 2

Tim Collins, retired farmer

Plate 3

Brendan McHale

Plate 4

Ted Tieman and Jeff Gouch

Plate 5

Joe Schum, blacksmith

Plate 6

Bernard Alblinger, mayor and hardware store owner

Volunteer fire department, Chief Don Tempel,
Bill Auth, Adam Auth, Mark Somers, Dave Martin

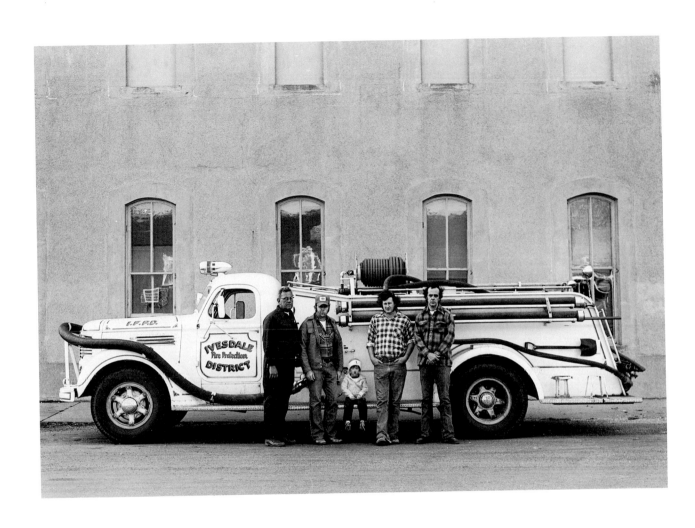

Plate 8

Gertie Flavin

Plate 9

Dennis Fuqua

Plate 10

Corner of Chapin and Johnson Streets

Plate 11

Justin O'Connor

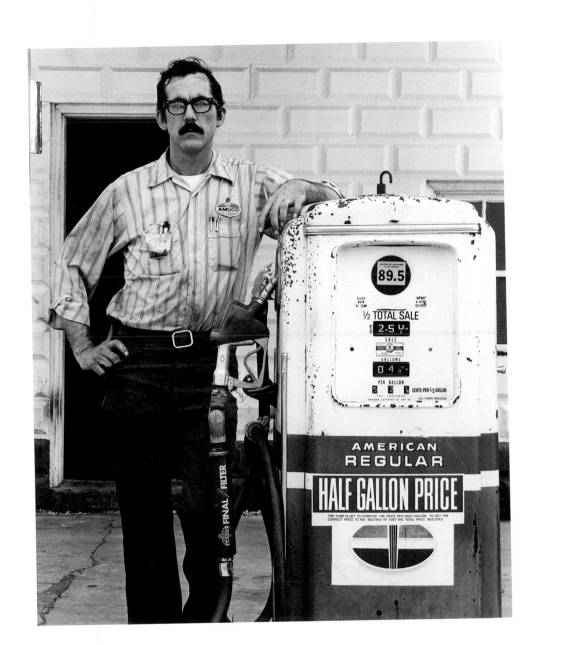

Plate 12

Rodney Jamison

Plate 13

Don Schum, welder

Plate 14

Sean Brennan

Plate 15

Mark Stoerger

Plate 16

Shannon Cheek

Plate 17

Knights of Columbus Hall and Ivesdale Inn,
Chapin Street

Plate 18

Father Marzolf

Plate 19

Charles Somers and Richard Flavin

Plate 20

Kathleen Piatt with son, James, and baby, Will,
at Sunday Mass

Plate 21

Joe Schum, at Sunday Mass

Plate 22

Irene Sullivan, rectory housekeeper

Plate 23

Gwen Bates

Plate 24

Clyde Manny, mail carrier

Plate 25

Chapin Street

Plate 26

Kirwan Cafe, Chapin Street

Plate 27

Irene Kirwan

Plate 28

Mason Harshbarger, Sue Crupper,
Barb Crupper, Eddie Pembroke, Scott Crowl,
Donny Fuqua

Plate 29

Chuck Crupper

Plate 30

Ivesdale Co-op

Plate 31

Mike Lawson, Co-op worker

Plate 32

Stanley Wright, Co-op worker

Plate 33

Wayne Debolt, Co-op worker

Plate 34

Lester Jamison, Co-op fertilizer
department manager

Plate 35

Wayne Phillips, Co-op worker

Plate 36

Tim Black and J. T. Sansare, Co-op workers

Plate 37

Rollin Busey, Co-op worker

Plate 38

Roger Thompson, Co-op worker

Plate 39

John Sebens, farm hand

Plate 40

Ervan Lowery, farmer

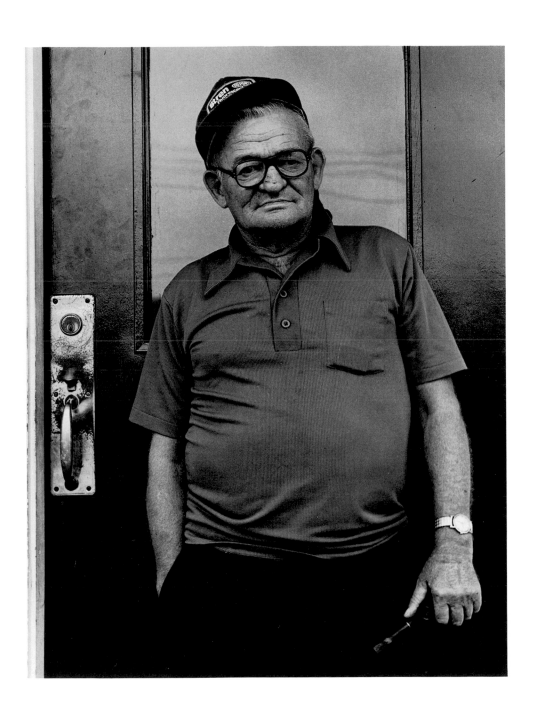

Plate 41

Frank and Kevin Alblinger, plumbers

Plate 42

Pat Feeny, farmer

Plate 43

George Cody, farmer

Plate 44

Nancy Auth, beautician

Plate 45

Pearl Hawkins

Plate 46

Junior McCoppin and Mike Jamison
at Tieman Tavern

Plate 47

Earl Guffey, Linda Schwartz, and
Richard Bialeschki at Ivesdale Inn

Plate 48

Ray Wood at Ivesdale Inn

Plate 49

Donna Sims

Plate 50

Jill Radmacher at St. Joseph Annual Costume
Contest and Wiener Roast

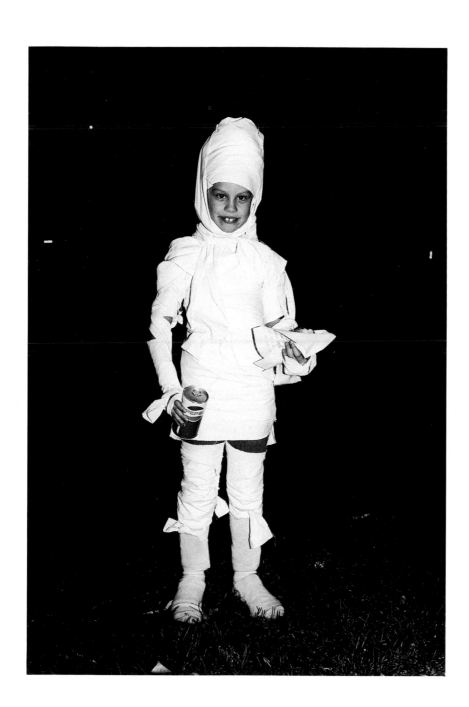

Plate 51

Theresa Tracy with daughter, Mary,
at St. Joseph Annual Costume Contest and
Wiener Roast

Plate 52

John Lewis at St. Joseph Annual Costume
Contest and Wiener Roast

Plate 53

Rilla Radmacher

Plate 54

Walter Hannon

Plate 55

Mike Hefferman, retired farmer

Plate 56

Robert and Mary Ellen Stoerger

Plate 57

McHale's home, Fourth Street

The photographs were made on Ilford Pan F film
with a Mamiya RB67 and Canon AE-1 and printed on
Ilford Ilfobrom paper by Raymond Bial.

The resulting prints were screened by Shanebrook Graphics,
Pontiac, Illinois, at 200 lines using an HCM DC-300 B Laser Scanner.
The resulting "double black" duotones thus retain as much as possible
of the tonal range of the originals.

Type and formatting by Four·C Typographers & Designers,
Champaign, Illinois.

Printing by Andromeda Printing & Graphic Arts,
Champaign, Illinois, on Warren's Cameo paper.